P9-DDV-138

POLAR ANIMALS
LIFE IN THE FREEZER

BELUGA WHALES

by Ruth Owen

WINDMILL
BOOKS™

New York

Published in 2013 by Windmill Books, An Imprint of Rosen Publishing
29 East 21st Street, New York, NY 10010

Produced for Windmill by Ruby Tuesday Books Ltd
Editor for Ruby Tuesday Books Ltd: Mark J. Sachner
US Editor: Sara Antill
Designer: Emma Randall
Consultant: Marianne Marcoux, PhD, Institute of Biological and Environmental Sciences, University of Aberdeen, Aberdeen, Scotland

Photo Credits:
Cover, 1, 4, 7, 10, 12–13, 14–15, 16–17, 18–19, 20 (top left), 20 (top right), 20 (bottom right), 21, 22–23, 24–25, 27, 28–29 © Shutterstock; 5 © Glenn Williams, National Institute of Standards and Technology; 8–9, 11 © FLPA; 20 (bottom left) © NOAA, B. Sheiko; 26 © Ansgar Walk.

Library of Congress Cataloging-in-Publication Data

Owen, Ruth, 1967–
Beluga whales / by Ruth Owen.
    p. cm. — (Polar animals: life in the freezer)
Includes index.
ISBN 978-1-4777-0221-5 (library binding) — ISBN 978-1-4777-0229-1 (pbk.) —
ISBN 978-1-4777-0230-7 (6-pack)
1. White whale—Juvenile literature. I. Title.
QL737.C433O945 2013
599.5'42—dc23
                                        2012026640

Manufactured in the United States of America

CPSIA Compliance Information: Batch # BW13WM: For Further Information contact Windmill Books, New York, New York at 1-866-478-0556

CONTENTS

SEA CANARIES

A group of tourists and scientists are listening to some strange sounds. They can hear whistles, chirps, and squeaks. Are the noises being made by a flock of excited birds?

No. The sounds are coming from underwater! The people are onboard a whale-watching boat, and they are hearing a group of beluga whales communicating with each other.

A beluga whale

The high-pitched, birdlike noises made by beluga whales gives them their nickname "sea canaries." Another name, "white whales," describes the color of their bodies.

Beluga whales are marine **mammals**. They belong to an animal group called **cetaceans**. This group includes porpoises, dolphins, and whales. Whales are divided into baleen whales and toothed whales. Baleen whales feed on tiny ocean creatures that they filter from the water in their huge mouths. Belugas and other toothed whales are **predators** that hunt for fish and other ocean animals.

The beluga whale's closest relative is the narwhal—another very unusual-looking type of whale! Male narwhals have a single, long, straight tusk that can grow to be nearly 10 feet (3 m) long.

Tusk

A group of four male narwhals

THE WORLD OF THE BELUGA WHALE

Beluga whales live in the Arctic Ocean and in its seas, including the Sea of Okhotsk, the Bering Sea, and Beaufort Sea.

Beluga whales spend time in the open ocean. They also live in coastal areas of Alaska, Canada, Greenland, Russia, and Norway. They spend time in bays and **estuaries**, and in inlets, the narrow bodies of water between small islands.

Sometimes belugas travel inland along major rivers, such as the Amur River in Russia and the Yukon River in Canada. They also spend time in the St. Lawrence River estuary in Canada.

WHERE BELUGA WHALES LIVE

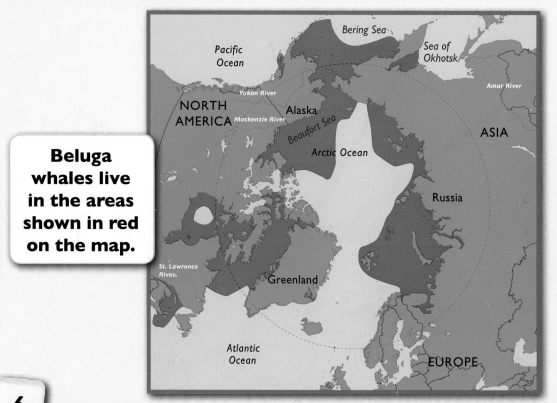

Beluga whales live in the areas shown in red on the map.

Some beluga whales live in the same area all year around. Others **migrate** thousands of miles (km) each year, living in one area in the summer and another in winter.

One large group, or **population**, of beluga whales lives in the Bering Sea in winter. In summer, the whales migrate over 3,000 miles (4,800 km) to the Mackenzie River estuary in Canada.

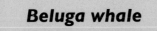

Beluga whale

The icy waters of the Arctic Ocean

THE BELUGA WHALE'S HABITAT

Beluga whales live in a variety of watery **habitats**. They are able to live in salt water and brackish water, which is a mixture of freshwater and salt water. They spend time in places where the water is very deep. They will also visit very shallow waters that only just cover their bodies.

When they are in the Arctic Ocean and its seas, the water temperature can be as low as 32 degrees Fahrenheit (0°C). The whales move from place to place searching for food, swimming among small icebergs and chunks of floating ice, called ice floes.

In summer, many belugas spend time in river mouths. Here, the water's temperature is higher than in the open seas because warmer water from inland is joining the ocean.

A small group of beluga whales swimming among ice floes

8

Beluga whales molt, or shed, their outer layer of old skin once a year in summer. During their molting season, the whales travel to areas where the water is very shallow. Then they rub their bodies in the gravel on thesea or riverbed to help remove the old skin.

Hundreds of beluga whales molting in an area of shallow water

BREATHING AND BLOWHOLES

Like all mammals, beluga whales must breathe air. As they swim, they regularly come to the surface to breathe.

Cetaceans, such as beluga whales, orcas, and dolphins, do not breathe through their mouths. They take in and let out air through a hole, called a blowhole, in the tops of their heads.

When diving in deep water to find food, beluga whales can stay underwater for up to 20 minutes without needing to come to the surface for air.

Sometimes beluga whales **forage** in places where over 90 percent of the ocean's surface is frozen. The whales swim underwater with a thick covering of ice above them. When they need to breathe, they have to find a small crack or hole in the ice. Then they pop up at this breathing hole and take in some air.

A beluga whale makes bubbles as it breathes out underwater.

Blowhole

A diver and a beluga whale swimming under the sea ice

Beluga whales can dive underwater to depths of 2,600 feet (800 m).

BELUGA BUDDIES

Beluga whales are very **social** animals. They travel, migrate, hunt for food, and spend their time in groups called pods.

A beluga whale pod is usually small with just two to ten members. Sometimes, however, hundreds of these pods may gather together in a larger herd.

Beluga whale calf

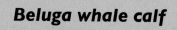

Adult beluga whale

The members of a beluga whale pod do not stay together all the time. Pods break up and then reunite. Males often travel together in male-only pods, while females with young will separate from other pods to spend time together.

As a pod moves through the ocean, the whales usually coordinate their breathing so that all the members of the group come to the surface to get air at the same time.

Scientists have seen huge herds of beluga whales with over 1,000 members!

PHYSICAL FACTS

To help them survive the cold in the icy **Arctic** waters where they live, beluga whales have a thick layer of fat, called blubber, on their bodies. This fatty insulation can be up to 4 inches (10 cm) thick.

Unlike a dolphin, orca, or other type of whale, this beluga whale can turn its head to look at the photographer taking its photo!

A beluga whale's body fat can make up around 50 percent of the animal's weight. Other types of whales, which live outside of Arctic waters, may only have around 20 percent of their body weight made up from fat.

Another way in which beluga whales are different from other cetaceans is that they have flexible necks and can move their heads. Beluga whales can nod their heads up and down and turn them from side to side.

Beluga whales grow to around 13 feet (4 m) long. Adults have an average weight of 1,100 to 1,500 pounds (500–700 kg).

TALKING BELUGA

Beluga whales aren't just very social. They are also very talkative! These whales make a large range of diffferent sounds.

Beluga whales sounds include whistles, birdlike chirps, squeals, clucks, mews, high-pitched trills, and noises that sound like bells.

The noises made by beluga whales can be so loud that it's possible for a person in a boat on the water's surface to hear the sounds coming from underwater.

No one knows what all this beluga talk means, but scientists think that mothers are probably communicating with their calves, and some sounds could be linked to **mating**. The animals may also be passing information to each other about food or enemies.

The sounds made by beluga whales are probably made in the animals' heads by the movement of air between air pockets, or sacs, near the blowhole.

A beluga whale mother and her calf

HUNTING WITH SOUND

In dark or murky waters, it's not always possible to see very far. This isn't a problem for beluga whales, however, because they are able to find and identify **prey** and other underwater objects using sound.

The melon

The whales send out a super-fast sequence of clicks into the water. The clicking sounds come from the large bulge on the whale's head, which is called the melon. The sounds bounce off objects in the water and travel back to the whale as echoes. The whale then picks up the echoes through its lower jaw. Next, the echoes are relayed to the whale's ears and to its brain, where the animal is able to decode the sounds.

The echoes can tell a whale the size, shape, and distance of an object. If the echoes pick up prey, such as a fish, the whale can even find out how fast the animal is moving! This method of using clicks and echoes to "see" objects using sound is called **echolocation**.

The clicks that a beluga whale sends out into the water when using echolocation can travel through the water at 1 mile per second (1.6 km/s).

WHAT'S ON THE MENU?

Beluga whales can spend up to 20 minutes underwater foraging for food. Most feeding dives, however, last for only two to five minutes.

Beluga whales hunt for fish such as herring, salmon, and cod. They also search for flatfish, such as flounder, which live on the seabed. Other ocean creatures on the beluga whale's menu include octopuses, squid, shrimp, clams, and crabs.

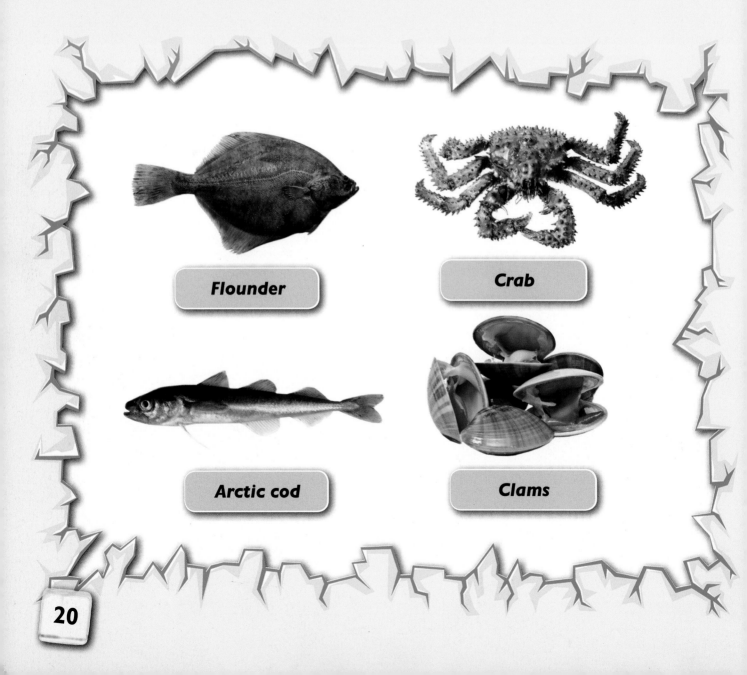

Flounder

Crab

Arctic cod

Clams

Sometimes several beluga whales will work together as a hunting team. They may drive, or chase, a shoal of fish from deep water into shallow water, where it is easier to catch them. They may also herd a large number of fish into one place. Then the whales can dive into the mass of fish to easily grab mouthfuls of their prey.

Beluga whales swallow ther prey whole. They use their small teeth for grabbing and holding prey, not for chewing.

BABY BELUGAS

Beluga whales mate in spring, from April to June. A female beluga is then pregnant for about 14 months and gives birth to a single calf the following year, in July or August.

Female beluga whales choose places to give birth and live with their young calves where the water is warmer and not too deep.

A calf feeding on milk

A newborn beluga calf is about 5 feet (1.5 m) long and can weigh up to 176 pounds (80 kg). The calf can swim as soon as it is born.

A beluga whale calf feeds on milk from its mother's body. When its teeth grow after about a year, it will begin to eat small fish and shrimp. However, the calf continues to drink milk until it is about two years old.

Calves learn how to hunt and avoid predators by watching older pod members. Young female whales learn how to care for calves by watching their mother and other older females.

Beluga whale calves are gray when they are born. Their skin gradually turns white during their first five or six years.

Mother beluga whale

PREDATORS

Beluga whales have just two natural predators—orcas and polar bears.

Orcas generally feed on belugas during the summer when the ocean is free of ice. In winter, orcas do not hunt beluga whales because there are ice sheets and ice floes in the water. Belugas do not have tall dorsal fins, so they are able to swim under the ice. The orca's dorsal fin, however, can be 3 feet (0.9 m) tall, making it difficult for orcas to chase belugas beneath the ice.

The beluga whale's other predator is the polar bear. Polar bears know that marine mammals, such as beluga whales and seals, must come to the surface to breathe air. A polar bear waits on the sea ice next to a breathing hole. When a beluga or seal surfaces to take a breath, the huge bear attacks, killing the animal by swiping at it and dragging it onto the ice.

An orca

Dorsal fin

Ridge

Instead of a dorsal fin, a beluga whale has a long, low ridge along its back.

A polar bear listens and watches for prey at a crack in the sea ice.

HUNTING BELUGA WHALES

Beluga whales have been hunted by Inuits and other native people in and around the Artic for many hundreds of years. The whales are still an important source of meat for many native communities today.

The hunting of beluga whales is carried out on a subsistence basis. This means that hunters only kill enough animals to fulfill their community's food needs.

The hunting of beluga whales must also be done in a way that is **sustainable** and does not reduce the animals' numbers too dramatically for the future. This is important because beluga whale numbers increase very slowly.

A young hunter is honored with a muktuk feast to celebrate his first beluga whale kill.

Inuits eat *muktuk*, a traditional food of whale skin with blubber attached, from beluga whales. The whales' blubber can also be made into oil for heating and lighting, and their skins are thick enough to be used as leather.

A female beluga whale will not have her first calf until she is around 10 years old. She will then have a baby every three years until she gets too old to reproduce. In a lifetime of 60 years, a female beluga whale may only raise around 10 calves.

THE FUTURE FOR BELUGA WHALES

While overhunting may not be a problem for beluga whales in most areas, they do still face many human-made dangers.

The fishing industry may take so many fish from the ocean that there are not enough for beluga whales to feed on.

Pollution, such as poisonous chemicals, and oil spills can damage the whales' watery habitat. Also, if the whales' prey is contaminated by pollution, dangerous levels of poisons may build up in the whales' bodies from the animals they eat.

Today, there are around 150,000 beluga whales in the world. Most beluga whale populations are stable, which means they are not dropping, and some populations are even increasing.

For the future, it's very important that we take care of beluga whales and their habitat so these unusual animals can enjoy life in the freezer for generations to come!

Many scientists are worried that high levels of noise pollution, from ships and oil-drilling activities in the ocean, may disturb and upset beluga whales. It might also affect their ability to communicate and use echolocation to **navigate** and find prey.

GLOSSARY

Arctic (ARK-tik)
The northernmost area on Earth, which includes northern parts of Europe, Asia, and North America, the Arctic Ocean, the polar ice cap, and the North Pole.

cetacean (sih-TAY-shun)
A member of the cetacean group of animals, which is made up of whales, dolphins, and porpoises. These animals are mammals that live in water.

echolocation
(eh-koh-loh-KAY-shun)
Sending out sounds that bounce off objects and create echoes that an animal, such as a beluga whale or dolphin, can use to create a picture of something that it cannot see with its eyes.

estuary (ES-choo-wer-ee)
A body of water on a coastline that has one or more rivers or streams flowing into it.

forage (FOR-ij)
To move from place to place looking for food.

habitat (HA-buh-tat)
The place where an animal or plant normally lives. A habitat may be a rain forest, the ocean, or a backyard.

mammal (MA-mul)
A warm-blooded animal that has a backbone and usually has hair, breathes air, and feeds milk to its young.

mating (MAYT-ing)
Coming together in order to have young.

migrate (MY-grayt)
To move to a new area for a period of time and then return. Animals may migrate to find food, to mate, or to avoid extreme weather.

navigate (NA-vuh-gayt)
To find and then travel a route from one place to another.

population (pop-yoo-LAY-shun)
The people or animals living in a particular place or area.

predator (PREH-duh-ter)
An animal that hunts and kills other animals for food.

prey (PRAY)
An animal that is hunted by another animal as food.

social (SOH-shul)
Liking to live with and be around others of one's kind.

sustainable (suh-STAY-nuh-bel)
Using resources in a way that can continue into the future.

Websites

For web resources related to the subject of this book, go to: www.windmillbooks.com/weblinks and select this book's title.

READ MORE

Antill, Sara. *A Whale's Life*. Living Large. New York: PowerKids Press, 2012.

Landau, Elaine. *Beluga Whales*. Animals of the Snow and Ice. Berkeley Heights, NJ: Enslow Publishers, 2010.

Nicklin, Flip, and Linda Nicklin. *Face to Face with Whales*. Face to Face with Animals. Des Moines, IA: National Geographic Children's Books, 2011.

INDEX